First published in 2002 by Watling St Publishing
The Old Chapel
East End
Northleach
Gloucestershire
GL54 3PQ

Printed in Thailand

ISBN 1-904153-02-X

24681097531

Cover design and illustration: Mark Davis
Cartoons: Martin Angel

GHOSTS, GHOULS AND PHANTOMS OF London

Travis Elborough

WATLING STREET

Travis Elborough is a freelance writer and lives in north London. He loves apple and stilton baguettes and enjoys playing Canasta.

This book is for Lauren

... and with thanks to Chris and Christine

Contents

London: The City Even the Dead Never Want to Leave

In the early 1970s a young man was making his way from Embankment underground station to the Strand. He decided to take a short cut by darting through Buckingham Street. He'd arranged to meet a friend for dinner at eight and was running slightly late. As he turned into the street, he peered at his watch. Eight twenty-six, it said. Oh well, what's ten, twenty minutes or so between friends? he thought. He quickened his step but was suddenly brought to an abrupt halt by a very peculiar sight. Staring down at him from the window of no. 12 Buckingham Street was a ghostly grey figure. The figure appeared to be wearing an old-fashioned wig – like the ones worn by judges – and was holding what looked like a large feather. The figure smiled at him, gave a slight nod of his head and then simply vanished.

The man shook his head, unable to understand quite what he had seen. He had been working too hard recently; perhaps he was just tired. The face of the figure had looked oddly familiar but he couldn't quite place it. As he drew closer to the house he noticed a blue plaque on the wall. It read: Samuel PEPYS (1633–1703), Diarist and Secretary of the Admiralty, lived here 1679-1688. Had he really just seen the ghost of the great London diarist and man about town, Samuel Pepys? He must have walked passed the plaque a hundred times and yet he'd never noticed it – or had he? Had his mind just stored it away and now decided to play a trick on him? He hurried away and tried to forget what he had seen. He later discovered that Pepys' ghost was a regular visitor to Buckingham St and had once even been spotted  strolling along nearby Villiers St near Charing Cross Station. It seems as though this particular Londoner just couldn't bear to leave the old place. As we shall discover, he is not alone...

What are Ghosts, Ghouls and Phantoms?

The simple, if useless, answer is we don't really know. Many people believe that when we die, a core part of us – some call it a spirit – lives on. Ghosts are thought by many to be spirits of the dead who, for some reason or another, are stuck on Earth. The spirit might have chosen to remain to contact a relative. Some people believe that if the departed has been murdered or died tragically he or she might be after justice or out for revenge.

Others think that ghosts could be echoes of the past, like constantly repeated old films. (Oh no, not *Ghostbusters* again!) Some are convinced that we ourselves produce them, or that our minds deceive us. The grouchy London writer Samuel Johnson (we'll meet him again later) felt it was impossible to say if ghosts existed or not. He once remarked that 'it is undecided whether or not there has ever been an instance of a spirit of any person appearing after death. All argument is against it; but all belief is for it.' Like Johnson, most of us rather like to believe in ghosts and we all love a really scary ghost story!

Whatever ghosts are they certainly come in many shapes and sizes. There are wispy figures that look like the long dead, hideous headless phantoms, screaming spooks, weird knocking noises and even just eerie icy sensations. (Isn't that just the weather?)

Speaking to Spooks

Spiritualists or mediums are people who think they can speak directly to the dead. They hold meetings or seances and using crystal balls or a device called a ouija board they try to contact them. One of the most famous mediums of all time and a leading figure in the Society for Psychical Research – a ghost-investigating organization – was based in London at the end of the 1800s. Her name was Madame Blavatsky. She was not the first mystic, fortune-teller or ghost-hunter to be drawn to the capital. London has always had a reputation for being a magical or haunted city. According to one legend, King Arthur and his wizard Merlin set up court in London. (I bet they used the Circle line! Get it! Round table, Circle Line!)

Spooky Streets

Given London's dark and bloody history it's not surprising that it has such a reputation for strange goings-on. Merciless monarchs, plagues, fires and wars have all ravaged it. You are never very far from the dead when you are in London. During the Black Death (a really revolting plague), hundreds of Londoners were buried in huge pits around the city. There were pits in Brompton, Hackney and Islington. Carnaby Street stands on top of an old plague pit. While the plague raged, ghosts were said to walk the streets among the living. (Everyone did look quite ill at the time. It was probably hard to spot the difference!)

London's streets are practically paved with blood. Brutal public executions were carried out on gallows where Marble Arch stands now. Disgruntled spirits and spooks seem to seep out of every corner of the capital. Ghosts have been spied in London's streets, churches, pubs, theatres and even on the Underground. (They feel happier six feet under!)

Books of the Dead

London's storybooks are jammed full of ghosts. The plays of **William Shakespeare** - who lived and worked in Southwark - are packed with ghosts. There are witches and ghost-daggers

in *Macbeth* and nasty old King Richard III is visited by a whole gang of ghosts. In the first productions of his spooky tragedy *Hamlet*, William himself played the ghost, 'doomed for certain term to walk the night'. (He was a ghost writer!)

Charles Dickens, perhaps London's best novelist, loved ghost stories. His most famous is *A Christmas Carol*. On Christmas Eve Ebenezer Scrooge, a miserable old miser, is haunted by the ghost of his old partner, Jacob Marley. Marley warns Scrooge to change his penny-pinching ways or he will be doomed to walk the earth in chains. Each time the bells of St Dunstan church (near Fleet Street) chime, Scrooge is visited by a different ghost: the ghosts of Christmas Past, Present and Future. You'll have to read for yourself to discover what happens ...

Stories about vampires – those blood-drinking phantoms who fear garlic, crucifixes and sunlight - first came from

Transylvania (now Romania) in Eastern Europe. In the 1300s Countess Erzebet Bathory of Hungary had a very unusual beauty cream. She murdered young girls and then bathed in their blood! She believed it kept her skin young. Erzebet was a real live countess but Count Dracula - fiction's finest bloodsucker – also came from Transylvania. However, in **Bram Stoker's** novel, the count abandons Transylvania to drink blood in London and sells his castle to buy houses in Piccadilly, Mile End, Bermondsey and in Purfleet – south of the Thames! (The commute was such a pain in the neck!)

The brilliant Scottish writer **Robert Louis Stevenson** – he wrote the classic adventure story *Treasure Island* - set his scariest tale in London. In *The Strange Case of Dr Jeckyll and Mr Hyde*, Dr Jeckyll makes a potion that turns him into the monster Mr Hyde. After drinking the potion Mr Hyde goes on the rampage in Soho and later turns back into Dr Jeckyll on a bench in Regent's Park.

And where but at London's King Cross Station – Platform 9 3/4 – could **Harry Potter** have begun his magical journey to Hogwarts School?

More spooky stuff has been written about London than anywhere else. Maybe it's because there is just more spooky stuff in London than anywhere else!

In this book we'll meet the city's foulest fiends, grimmest ghouls, strangest spectres and funniest phantoms. Some of the stories have become blurred in the mists of time or exaggerated over the years - so keep your eyes open and your wits about you. Things are about to get spooky. It's time to get into some ghostly gear and then it's off to the Tower of London.

A Capital Kit for Ghost Hunters

Clothes
Never go ghost hunting in the nude! It scares the ghosts away.

A woolly hat
In the winter ghost-hunters should always wear a woolly hat, preferably one with earflaps. If things get too scary you can pull it down over your eyes!

An Anorak
A ghost-hunter must try to look as normal as possible. Some spooks just hate being stalked, so

few will suspect that anyone wearing an anorak is after them.

Finish off your ghost-hunting outfit with a thick woollen cardigan or a tank top. If you wear glasses make sure you put a bit of sticky plaster on one of the arms.

Some ghost-hunters swear that odd socks always bring them luck. Why not try odd shoes or even wearing different-coloured gloves.

A-Z of London
The essential item for the London ghost-hunter. Always handy to know where you are and how to get to where you want to go; especially if you are off to Spirit Quay or Bleeding Heart Lane.

A Notebook and Pencil
To scribble down any odd things you see, or to draw rude pictures of people you see on the Tube.

A Torch
Ghosts seem to favour the night. So always take a torch with you if you are ghost-hunting after dark. Why not give your friends a fright by shining the

torch under your chin and pulling a hideous face!

A Camera
A camera fitted with a flash is essential for snapping any spooks you spot. Keep quiet about this but ... if you have a camera that takes 35mm films, you can even fake your own ghost photos! After you've finished a film, rewind it and put it back into the camera. Use it again. When you get the pictures developed they'll be what's called double-exposed. There will be spooky double images on each picture!

A Tape Recorder
Just in case you come across any strange sounds or eerie echoes. You can also use it to create spooky sounds of your own. Try moaning or screaming into the microphone or find a squeaky door or creaking floorboard to record.

This book ... (Well done!)

Why not buy extra copies for your friends, cousins, pets and plants. It's marvellous for propping up desks and wedging doors open. Buy six and use them as an attractive set of coasters. Oh ... and it's a great read.

CHAPTER ONE

Head over Heels

A Choice of Toppings at The Tower of London

The Tower of London was built by William the Conqueror as a fortress. It wasn't long before it became notorious as a royal prison and place of execution. Over the centuries, kings, queens, princes, princesses, lords, ladies, priests and plotters have all been imprisoned, tortured and executed within its walls. Two young royal princes mysteriously vanished from the Tower, never to be seen again.

Only posh people were beheaded – poor people had to make do with being hanged! The reason? Ropes were cheaper than axes! Most nobles had their heads severed on Tower Hill or on Tower Green. Their headless phantoms are among the variety of ghosts who stalk almost every corner of the Tower.

Unlucky Anne Boleyn

Anne Boleyn was Henry VIII's second wife. Henry had married Anne so that she could give him a baby boy; he desperately wanted a son to rule after him. He had already divorced his first wife, Catherine of Aragon, because she had failed to produce a boy. Anne gave birth to a girl. Henry was not very pleased. (Little did he know that their daughter would grow up to become Queen Elizabeth I - one of England's greatest rulers.) Henry decided he'd had enough of Anne and wanted a new queen. He had a gander about the royal court and spotted a nice-looking girl called Jane Seymour. He sent her jewels and flowers and declared his undying love for her. She was flattered. Before long the pair were seen strolling about the palace arm in arm. There was just one snag. Henry was still married to Anne. Henry cooked up a scam to get rid of her. He accused Anne of having other boyfriends and had her sentenced to death. How unfair was that? He had done the wandering, not Anne.

When Anne had been crowned as Henry's Queen, a magnificent barge had brought her along the Thames to the Tower. Now, just three years later, she was making exactly the same journey. This time she was going to lose her head, not have a flashy crown plonked on top of it. She entered the Tower through Traitor's Gate - a grim iron gateway. Henry always had Traitor's Gate decorated with festering severed heads. (He thought they brightened the place up.) For Anne they were a chilling hint of her own fate. A swordsman was specially brought over from Calais in France to behead her. On 19 May 1536 Anne was led out on to Tower Green. Trembling with fear she knelt down and her head was lopped off with a single blow.

On misty mornings Anne's headless ghost, dressed all in white, has been seen floating near the Bloody Tower. All who see her claim to feel an overbearing sense of sadness.

Wandering Wally

Sir Walter Raleigh is famous for sailing around the world and bringing potatoes and tobacco to England. (Imagine life before chips!) He also spent years imprisoned in the Tower of London.

Walter had been one of Queen Elizabeth I's favourites. Lizzie loved Wally. He was a dishy explorer who enchanted her with accounts of his daring adventures. He'd go off to sea for months on end and then return loaded with great gifts for her. (He was like Father Christmas and Hans Solo from *Star Wars* all rolled into one.)

When Elizabeth died and James I of England came to the throne Wally knew his luck had run out. James hated smoking and he thought potatoes tasted horrible. He blamed Wally for bringing them to Britain and wasted no time in putting him in the Tower. Wally remained there for the next eleven years.

Wally was finally released after persuading James that he could find El Dorado, the fabled city of gold. El Dorado was believed to be in the heart of the Amazon Jungle in South America. It was supposed to have so much gold that its king used gold dust instead of talcum powder! Wally sailed to

America promising to return with a fortune for James. The voyage was a fiasco. He came back to England empty-handed. The King was livid. Wally was flung back into the Tower and promptly sentenced to death. He was beheaded not at Tower Green but in Westminster. His ghost, however, seems to prefer the Tower. He has been sighted happily strolling along its ramparts, just as he had done when he was imprisoned there.

Guards report that there is a distinct whiff of tobacco smoke in the air whenever he walks by. He obviously hasn't kicked the habit yet!

Headless of Holland Park

Holland Park in West London is named after Lord Henry Rich, the Earl of Holland. As you might have guessed, Lord Henry and his wife, Lady Rich, had stacks of cash. They lived in a glorious mansion called Holland House. In the Second World War much of the house was destroyed by bombs but what is left is haunted by the Earl's ghost.

Lord Henry was a close friend of King Charles I. Charles was quite a lazy king and wasn't very keen on governing. He much preferred playing tennis or having his picture painted. The people disliked his Queen Henrietta Maria; she was French and a Catholic (not good things to be in 17th-century England). The government felt Henrietta had too much power over the King. A row broke out between the King and the government. This escalated into the full-blown Civil War. The country was divided between the Roundheads or Parliamentarians led by Oliver Cromwell, who were against the king, and the Royalists, or Cavaliers, who remained loyal to Charles.

Henry was in charge of the Cavalier forces in London. In 1648 he led an army of 500 Cavaliers in a final bid to win control of the city. Henry was Charles' last hope. If he could capture London there was every chance Oliver's Roundheads would crumble and Charles could retake the throne in triumph. If Henry failed it would all be over for Charles. Everything depended on Henry.

Oh dear.

Sadly for Charles Henry was a terrible general. His troops were well and truly thrashed in a battle on Surbiton Common. The Cavaliers had lost. Charles was beheaded and so was Henry. (They were head-hunted by the new government!)

If Henry was a hopeless general he's even more useless as a ghost. No surprise spooking for Henry – he always gives plenty of advance warning when he is going to haunt.

There used to be an old wooden panel in the hallway of Holland House. When Henry's ghost was going to visit he left three great trickles of blood on the woodwork. (Hell to wipe off and not a very subtle way of saying ' Cooee! I am going to haunt tonight'.) The wooden panel was really a hidden door. At midnight the panel slid open and out strode Henry, carrying his head under his arm and trying to look as frightening as possible. The panel was destroyed in the war but this doesn't stop Henry haunting the house. If you do see him try to look surprised and please don't laugh - he's only doing his best!

The Spectral Servant of St James's Palace

Our next ghost does have a head on its shoulders but only just...

On 31 May 1810 it was the scene of a grisly murder ... Read all about it over the page ...

The Daily Beast

Grub Street's Greediest Animal

June 1810, 1 penny

Servant Slashed at St James's

Confused stories are still emerging about a dreadful murder at St James's Palace, the home of King George III's son, Ernest Augustus the Duke of Cumberland, writes William Boot. At about eleven o'clock last night, 31 May 1810, the very bloody corpse of Sallis, the Duke of Cumberland's manservant, was found in the servants' quarters. An hour before a horrific noise had been heard coming from the Duke's bedroom. One palace source claimed that the Duke had stumbled out covered in blood and carrying his sword. The Duke is then reported to have begged his servants to fetch him a doctor, telling them that someone had crept into his room and tried to kill him. He'd fought the attacker off but in the scuffle had been stabbed in the leg. The attacker had then fled into the night, he said.

When the doctor arrived

to examine the Duke's wound he found only a tiny scratch. The doctor was said to be puzzled about how such a little cut had produced so much blood. It was then that the body of Sallis, the Duke's manservant, was discovered. His throat had been slashed and a cut-throat razor lay by his bloody body. The cut was so deep that his head was nearly severed from his body. The doctor is on record as saying that only a sword could have made such a gash. No member of the royal household was available for comment. An inquest is expected in the next few days. We hope to have more on this staggering story soon.

An inquest was held. The team of judges – many of whom were close friends of the royal family – decided that Sallis must have attacked his master and then committed suicide. Not everyone was convinced. How could Sallis have sliced his own neck so severely? Shaving? Rumours of a right royal cover-up began to spread. Some claimed that the Duke had been trying it on with Sallis's daughter and Sallis had not been very happy about it.

Had the Duke killed his servant after a row and got his friends in high places to hush the incident up? The truth will never been known. By July the papers were dominated by the news of a dockers' strike and the incident was soon forgotten.

It was just another murder in an age when public hangings were still London's most popular form of free entertainment.

On quiet evenings St James's Palace receives an unpleasant reminder. Sallis's hideous ghost walks through its corridors leaving a stench of congealed blood behind him. Lovely!

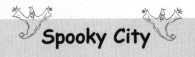

Spooky City

St James's Palace in Pall Mall has a rather grim history ...

It was built by Henry VIII on the site of an old leper colony. Leprosy is a disgusting disease that causes bits of skin and even fingers and toes to fall off.

Henry's daughter, the equally murderous monarch Queen 'Bloody' Mary, died in St James's.

After he had been beheaded, King Charles I's corpse was brought to St James's Palace and prepared for burial. It was here that his head was actually stitched back onto his body!

CHAPTER TWO

Bewildering Beasts and Animal Apparitions

The Bear at the Tower of London

The Tower of London's most terrifying spook is not a headless figure or a hooded monk but an animal: the ghost of a gigantic bear. The ghost bear was last seen by one of the Tower's guards. The guard was patrolling the area by the Martin Tower when he suddenly came face to face with a gigantic and extremely angry-looking bear. As the bear loomed towards him he tried to spear it with the bayonet of his rifle. The blade passed straight through the beast and stuck into the tower's wooden door. He fainted in shock and when he regained consciousness, the bear had vanished. Two days later he died.

Wild bears were once common in England and were used for entertainment. Large crowds used to gather to watch bears fight dogs in bear-baiting contests. (It was certainly livelier than snooker.) During the 16th century it was London's most popular sport. Queen Elizabeth I was a huge fan. She would take visiting nobles to bear-baiting matches at an arena in Southwark, near present-day London Bridge. The Tower of London had its own bear-baiting pit. The ghost could well belong to a bear that died in one of the Tower's fights.

Spooky City

The Tower wasn't just the place where enemies of the Crown went to have their heads chopped off. Until 1834 it was also the home of the royal zoo.

The zoo was started by Henry III in 1235 when the Emperor Frederick II of Germany sent him three leopards as a gift. Exotic animals must have been Henry's favourite kind of present because a few years later the King of Norway gave him a polar bear. Henry, however, wasn't so generous to ordinary Londoners. He ordered that they should pay for the bear's food and its muzzle and chain. In return they were able to watch it fishing in the Thames.

Fighting bears aren't the only animal apparitions. Our next spook is a fowl vision in white ...

Francis Bacon and the Phantom Frozen Chicken of Highgate

Sir Francis Bacon was a brilliant poet, scientist, politician and judge who lived in London 400 years ago. Bacon was so talented that some people believe that he rather than William Shakespeare wrote plays such as *Hamlet* and *Romeo and Juliet*.

Francis was an advisor to both Queen Elizabeth I and her successor King James I but his glittering political career came to an abrupt end in 1621. He was found guilty of accepting bribes and flung into the Tower of London. Francis was ruined. Eventually he was only imprisoned for three days but he was banished from James's Court and many of his old friends refused to speak to him. Despite this he wasn't too miserable. He now had plenty of time to study. He busied himself by reading, writing and conducting scientific experiments. One particular experiment proved to be his final undoing.

On a bitterly cold day in the spring of 1626, Francis was travelling through Highgate Village. The ground was covered with snow and the horses pulling his carriage slipped, jolting Bacon from his thoughts. He leant out of the window to see what was going on and noticed something quite extraordinary. Where the coaches' wheels had disturbed the snow the grass underneath looked fresh and green. The snow seemed somehow to preserve the grass.

He suddenly wondered if food or meat could be preserved in the same way.

An experiment was hastily arranged. He ordered his coachman to stop at a local farm and buy a chicken. The unlucky bird was then killed by the roadside, plucked, stuffed full of snow and placed in a bag full of ice. Francis was so busy creating the world's first frozen chicken that he forgot to put his coat on. The weather was now absolutely freezing and he collapsed, shivering with cold. A friend of his lived nearby and he was carried to his house and put to bed. At 65 years of age Bacon was no spring chicken. (Groan!) He was just too old and weak to shake off the chill. The cold quickly turned into a fever and he died just a few days later.

After his death a rather unusual apparition began to appear in what is now Highgate's Pond Square. A huge ghostly white bird has been seen flapping its wings, squawking and running around before evaporating into thin air. Could the ghost belong to that of Bacon's unfortunate victim?

Spooky City

Once the only place to be seen dead in,
Highgate Cemetery, with its shattered
tombs and overgrown ivy, is London's
spookiest graveyard. From black masses -
evil satanic ceremonies - and animal
sacrifices to exorcisms and vampire hunts,
some very scary things have happened
here. Ghosts and ghouls can't get enough of
the old place. There have be sightings of
wispy white figures, demonic black dogs
and shadowy monks making their way
through the graveyard.

The political thinker Karl Marx, the
novelist George Eliot and the Victorian
magician David Devant are all buried at
Highgate. While Karl and George prefer
the quiet death, David's devious ghost is
thought to hover in Swain's Lane, the road
that runs beside the cemetery. On one
occasion he is supposed to have knocked a
cyclist off a bike with his top hat. He was
only looking for his rabbit.

The Black Dog of Newgate Prison

Newgate was London's most notorious and most disgusting prison. For nearly 800 years it stood where The Old Bailey - our largest law court - stands today, in the City (the home of London's biggest businesses). From its earliest days it was famed for being a stinking, horrible place. The smell was so bad that for centuries it polluted the whole surrounding area. Visitors to the prison had to cover their noses with handkerchiefs soaked in vinegar to avoid being sick.

The most unfortunate prisoners were chained at the ankles and cast into dank underground dungeons. Food was scarce and any scraps available were thrown into them. The prisoners then had to scrabble around in the dark to find their meagre rations. Even cells that were above ground were dirty and overcrowded. Sickness and disease were always raging through the prison. In 1419 an outbreak of a hideous illness - called Gaol Fever - killed 64 prisoners and the gaol's keeper. As if things weren't bad enough, a sinister and very smelly ghost also haunted the prison. According to legend, the ghost first appeared shortly after one prisoner came to a particularly gruesome end ...

In 1270, during the reign of King Henry III, London was struck by a terrible famine. Many died of starvation. In Newgate one group of prisoners hit on a dastardly plan to ease their aching bellies. They killed a man who had just arrived, roasted him over a fire and gleefully tucked into his flesh. Unbeknown to them their victim was a wizard who had been imprisoned for sorcery. (Harry Potter, eat your heart out! Err, on second thoughts, perhaps not ...) No sooner had the gang finished stuffing their faces than a huge, foul, black hound appeared. Its eyes gleamed like fire and its fangs dripped with blood. The devilish dog wasted no time in tearing them apart. It then sat down to wolf up their dismembered limbs. Having avenged the wizard's murder it disappeared as swiftly as it had arrived.

On the nights before executions the monstrous black dog would return. Its shambling shape was regularly seen prowling the prison yard, a sign that death was near. Its appearance was always accompanied by the stench of rotting meat.

Newgate was demolished in 1902 but the haunting goes on. The fiendish black dog has been spotted pacing across a courtyard where part of the prison used to stand.

CHAPTER THREE

Poltergeists and Things that Go Bump in the Night

The word 'poltergeist' comes from the German for noisy or restless spirits. This particular type of ghost earned its name because it makes its presence felt by banging and crashing about. Poltergeists have been known to slam doors, shut windows and move, and sometimes break, objects. Usually poltergeists are playful, mischievous spirits but the odd one has been known to turn nasty.

Spooky City

In August 1977 a house in Enfield, North London, began to be plagued by a violent poltergeist. The noisy spirit threw chairs around, rocked chests of draws, hurled marbles and made terrible crashing and knocking noises. The poltergeist seemed to focus on a teenage girl called Janet. The family were so frightened they called in a psychic detective to investigate.

The detective was pelted with marbles by the poltergeist the moment he stepped into the house. He saw doors mysteriously fly open. He found that his cameras and tape recorders would fuse whenever he tried to record the phantom. By now an extraordinarily deep voice was heard coming from Janet's mouth. Janet claimed to have no control over the voice and would fall into a trance when it spoke. On one occasion the spirit appeared to throw her violently into the air.

The poltergeist made the front pages of the newspapers on 10 September 1977. Reporters and investigators flocked to the house. For the next two years the awful disturbances continued and then they stopped almost as abruptly as they had begun. No one knows what caused the strange events or why they stopped so suddenly.

Amid the hustle and bustle of life in the capital you might think that no one would even notice the knockings of a disgruntled ghost. One London poltergeist, however, caused such a stir that huge crowds gathered to witness it. The city's most famous – and sceptical – writer was called in to investigate.

Dr Johnson and the Curious Case of Scratching Fanny of Cock Lane

Number 33 Cock Lane, Smithfield, was the home of Richard Parsons, a clerk at the nearby church of St Sepulchre's, his wife, Mrs Parsons, and their twelve-year-old daughter, Elizabeth. Our tale begins in spring 1759 when Richard let rooms out to an elegant and respectable-looking couple, Mr William Kent and his wife Fanny.

At first the landlord and his lodgers got on well. So well, in fact, that (rather unusually) William lent Richard some money. It wasn't long before Richard discovered that Mr and Mrs Kent were not really married. Fanny was actually William's sister-in-law. Explain that one! William's first wife (Fanny's sister) had been very ill. The couple had become close and fallen in love when they were nursing (the real) Mrs Kent. However, the law in those days would not allow them to marry (it was believed they were as good as brother and sister). And in those days it was disgraceful for a man and woman to live together without being married. Landlords usually refused to take unmarried tenants.

But Richard felt sorry for William and Fanny, they appeared to care deeply for each other and so he decided to let them stay.

Richard started to feel uneasy when William told him about a peculiar legal arrangement. As they had been unable to marry, the couple had made out their last will and testament. If Fanny died William would inherit all her money and vice versa. This struck Richard as a little odd but he didn't worry about it too much.

One night, while William was away on business, Fanny and Elizabeth, Richard's daughter, were woken up by an awful noise. Fanny had been feeling lonely and as there had been a chill in the air she and Elizabeth had decided to share a bed. Snuggled up beneath the sheets and blankets, they'd felt cosy and secure. Imagine their horror when a piercing, scratching sound began to reverberate about the bedroom. The noise seemed to come from beneath their bed. They peered under it. There was nothing there. They tore off the covers. Again there was nothing. Fanny fled the room in tears. The atrocious noise carried on throughout the night. The next night it returned. Richard was convinced it was coming from the shoemaker who lived next door. The neighbour denied having anything to do with it. For the rest of the week the scratching continued.

When William returned, he decided they had to leave the house. He asked Richard to repay his loan. Richard refused. He was losing two tenants as it was. How could he be expected to pay William back? There were angry scenes. William and Fanny packed up their belongings and stormed out and they moved to a new home in Clerkenwell. The scratching had terrified Fanny; she had not slept for days and was exhausted. Shortly after leaving Cock Lane she fell mysteriously ill. She developed a raging temperature and kept falling asleep only to wake up bathed in sweat. She had dreadful nightmares about her dead sister. Fanny was sure that her sister had been trying to contact her from the grave. She believed the scratching was a sign that she too was going to die. Her premonition proved alarmingly accurate: a month later Fanny was dead.

Once William and Fanny had left Richard's house the scratching had stopped and Cock Lane had returned to normal. No sooner had Fanny died than it started all over again. This time the scratching shadowed Elizabeth. Wherever she sat or

37

slept the eerie din followed. The noises even followed her when she left the house - like a ghostly ghettoblaster. A local nurse who came to examine Elizabeth decided to try and communicate with the spectre. With Richard's help she asked it a series of questions, telling the ghost to scratch once for yes and twice for no. Knock, knock! Who's there? The ghost claimed to be Fanny and said that William had poisoned her with arsenic.

Spooky City

Cock Lane leads into Smithfield, London's meat market. Animals aren't the only creatures to have been butchered here. Smithfield was the site of hundreds of grisly public executions. Queen Mary Tudor had over 200 Protestants burnt at the stake at Smithfield. (Barbecued bishop, anyone?) Mary killed so many people that she became known as Bloody Mary. Some mornings, if there is a light breeze, the air is filled with the acrid smell of burning flesh.

News of these unearthly events spread quickly. People thronged to Cock Lane. Richard charged visitors 6 pence a time to hear Fanny's ghost. William was furious. He denied murdering Fanny. He maintained that Richard was nothing but a lying cheapskate who'd only invented the ghost to avoid paying his loan back and was making a tidy profit out of the spook to boot. This only fuelled interest. The queues outside Richard's house got so unruly that the city's authorities decided to investigate the matter. The man they chose to lead the inquiry was Dr Samuel Johnson.

Dr Johnson was one of the leading figures in the London of George III (the mad king). He was a writer, critic and playwright. He compiled the first English dictionary and a complete edition of Shakespeare's plays. He was a hard man to impress. And he was no oil painting either! One of his eyes was wonky, he didn't wash, and his wigs, which didn't fit him, were always singed on one side where he read by candlelight. Johnson was the perfect person to look into these very strange goings on.

The ghost announced that it would knock on the lid of Fanny's coffin to prove that it was telling the truth. Johnson and his team met Richard and Elizabeth at St John's Church in Clerkenwell. They descended a set of smelly damp steps into the cobweb-strewn crypt where Fanny's body lay buried. With only candlelight (watch out for that wig, Johnson!) to guide them, the party carefully tiptoed through the gloom. Elizabeth trembled with fear; here she was standing face to face with the icy tomb of a woman who only a few months earlier she had cuddled for warmth. That night the ghost remained silent.

Johnson declared the whole thing was a sham. He accused Elizabeth of faking the noises. Elizabeth was searched and a small wooden board was found hidden under her dress. If the board was tapped it made a scratching sound.

Johnson had been right. The ghost was a fraud. Richard had forced his own daughter to fake it, all so he could make a few quid and get out of paying William back. What a rotter! He was charged with slandering William. He swore he was innocent but it was no good. He was found guilty and sent to prison for two years. Strangely, although Elizabeth had been caught red-handed, he always maintained that the ghost had been real.

Nearly a century after his death something happened that might have proved Richard was telling the truth after all.

In the 1820s St John's Church was being rebuilt. It was decided that the coffins in the crypt should be removed during the building work. As the workmen went about this spooky task they noticed that one coffin was curiously stained. They opened it up. Staring out at them was the perfectly preserved face of a young woman. Petrified, they quickly shut it up again and placed it with the others.

There is one substance that can stain coffins and stops bodies from rotting away. It is the poison arsenic. Was the body

Fanny's corpse? And, if so, did William really kill Fanny and his wife? Not everyone believes the story and unfortunately we may now never know. In 1941, during the London Blitz, a bomb devastated the church. When the rubble was cleared there was no trace of Fanny's coffin.

Spooky City

A shop in the Burlington Arcade in Piccadilly was once pestered by a mischievous poltergeist. The poltergeist, whom the staff called Percy, loved playing with the display of handbags. Each morning the staff would arrive to discover the bags scattered all over the floor or perched at bizarre angles on the till. The shop's owner got so fed up she stopped stocking handbags! There's never been a peak out of Percy since.

CHAPTER FOUR

Haunting Highwaymen

In the 1600s and 1700s, highwaymen (and women) plagued the roads in and out of London. In Kensington and Knightsbridge – now posh parts of town, then villages on the outskirts of the city - highwaymen were so common it was dangerous to go out after dark. (Unless of course you were a highwayman in which case you could catch up with the latest highway robbery gossip.) Coaches and horsemen were regularly held up in the green fields and heaths of Finchley, Hampstead, Highgate, Wimbledon and Putney.

Stories of their daring robberies captured the public's imagination. Their deeds were widely celebrated in books and songs of the time. Some highwaymen really were chivalrous 'gentlemen of the road' but many were just thugs who preyed on vulnerable travellers. With the theft of anything worth more than a shilling punishable by death, most ended up swinging from the gallows at Tyburn (now Marble Arch). The ghosts of two of the most notorious highwaymen frequently return to their old stomping grounds.

Dastardly Dick Turpin

A shadowy figure, wearing an old-fashioned three-cornered hat, astride a majestic black horse, has been seen galloping over Hampstead Heath. Could the mysterious ghostly horseman be none other than the dastardly highwayman, Dick Turpin?

Dick Turpin is the most famous highwayman of all time. Usually regarded as a dashing romantic hero, Turpin was actually pretty ugly. He was short, hairy and his face was scarred by smallpox, a hideous disease that causes the skin to break out in pus-filled pimples. Dick was also a useless shot – during one raid he accidentally shot and killed one of his own gang.

Dick was born in a pub in Essex. He was trained as a butcher but began to steal cattle in Plaistow, East London. It wasn't long before Dick had branched out into burglary and highway robbery. (Cattle do get a bit whiffy after a while!) Teaming up with Robert King, he conducted raids on coaches on the highroads of Essex and on Finchley Common and Hampstead Heath.

A reward of £200 – a small fortune in those days – was offered for his capture. After a series of narrow escapes he decided to lie low and moved to Yorkshire (he liked the puddings). Here he was caught stealing horses and hanged.

Though he was hanged in York Dick Turpin returns to London for haunting. His horses' hooves have also been heard echoing around the old stables of a pub he drank at in Hampstead. The pub – The Spaniard – is still in use today. (Ask Mum or Dad to try their whines and spirits!)

Spooky City

Parliament Hill on Hampstead Heath earned its name because it was where Guy Fawkes and his fellow Gunpowder Plotters were going to meet and watch the Houses of Parliament burn down. Guy was the explosives expert. His job was to hide under the Houses of Parliament, light the fuse and then make his way to Hampstead to join the others. The dastardly plot was foiled when Guy, fuse in hand, was discovered in Parliament's cellars.

Each year on Bonfire Night, as the fireworks fizz and fly, the forlorn ghosts of the conspirators return to Parliament Hill. Five spooky horsemen are said to ride to the highest point and gaze down on over London. Their eyes are still desperately straining to catch a glimpse of Parliament in flames.

Jerry Abershaw

Wimbledon Common is graced by the ghostly gallops of another highwayman: Jerry Abershaw. Jerry was just seventeen when he became a highwayman and he was executed at the ripe old age of twenty-two. In his short career he terrorized South London. He led a vicious gang who robbed the roads between Wimbledon and Putney. He was caught after killing a member of the Bow Street Runners (London's first police force) in a tavern in Southwark. He showed no remorse for his crimes and even laughed and put his hat on when the judge sentenced him to death.

While he was waiting to be hanged Jerry used cherry juice to graffiti the walls of his prison cell (Jerry woz 'ere).

Jerry's mother had once told him that if didn't stop stealing he would die with his boots on (rather than in slippers in a quiet nursing home in Worthing). When he arrived at the gallows in Kennington he kicked off his boots just to prove her wrong. As a warning to others his dead body was bound in chains and hung on a post (called a gibbet) on Wimbledon Hill. A horse's gallops followed by a cry of 'Stand and Deliver!' are heard there to this day.

CHAPTER FIVE

Mournful Monks and Melancholy Figures

Ghostly shrouded figures are as much of a feature of London as red buses and scrawny pigeons. Their spooky forms have been seen in the dilapidated edges of Highgate Cemetery, by St Paul's Cathedral and strolling along the south bank of the Thames. These spectres seem to be doomed to keep a constant watch over the streets and churchyards they knew in their lifetimes.

The Ghostly Monks of Greyfriars

Christ Church on Newgate Street in the City of London was built by Sir Christopher Wren – the architect who also designed St Paul's Cathedral. Christ Church was constructed on the old home of a group of Franciscan monks - called the Grey Friars. Yes, you guessed it, they wore grey-coloured robes. How they kept their robes grey is other matter. Just opposite their priory there was a meat market called the Shambles – probably because it was one. Rancid gore from rotting animal carcasses littered the whole street. It was truly disgusting. The monks - who wore sandals - had to tiptoe through this muck to get into their church. They would have been splattered with blood almost every day. Perhaps they should have been renamed the Grey and Red Friars!

All that now remains of the church is its steeple, a ruined wall and the graveyard, which has been turned into a garden. It is in this garden that hooded spectres have been spied. A row of ghostly monks, their heads bowed in prayer, are reported to drift slowly across the lawn. Their ghosts are said to calm, rather than frighten, anyone who sees them. In the 1300s over a hundred monks died here in the revolting plague called the Black Death. Do these ghosts belong to those unfortunate victims? What else would make them want to stay inside the ruins of the old church? Could it be that they just don't want to go outside and get their robes dirty?

The Black Nun of The Bank of England

The Bank of England in the City of London is nicknamed the Old Lady of Threadneedle Street. The origins of the nickname are now shrouded in mystery but some people believe that the ghost who haunts the bank inspired it.

The ghost is thought to be Sarah Whitehead. In the 1820s Sarah lived in London with her older brother Peter. When they were children Peter was always getting into scrapes. Whether it

was misbehaving at the dinner table or tormenting the family dog, Peter was always up to some kind of mischief. Sarah was more sensible but sensitive and a bit fragile. Peter looked after his sister. She in turn adored her brother and the pair were inseparable. As Peter grew up he calmed down and got a job working at the Bank of England as a cashier. He was earning a good wage, so the pair set up home together. Sarah devoted herself to the house while her brother toiled at the bank.

Peter quickly grew bored of the bank. Where was the fun in spending day after day crouched over a desk? He was young and wanted to enjoy himself. He started to spend more of his evenings in the pub. He took up gambling and started hanging out with a girl who wore far too much make-up. He got lazy at work, constantly arriving late. He lost files, left wads of notes lying on the counter and forgot to reply to letters. Eventually he was asked to resign. By now he was heavily in debt. He began forging cheques to pay his bills. He was caught and sentenced to death for fraud.

Sarah was blissfully unaware of her brother's fate. After resigning Peter had continued to pretend to his sister that he worked at the bank. Friends had been too frightened to tell her the truth. To explain his disappearance they claimed he had gone abroad on business. After a week or so, though, Sarah became suspicious. She went to the bank to find out where he was.

Spooky City

In London during the 1700s corpses were literally worth their weight in gold. Doctors and surgeons, keen to find out how human beings ticked, paid grave-robbers for fresh bodies to dissect. The bigger the body, the more the grave-robbers earned.

A cashier at the Bank of England, who was over seven feet tall, was so frightened of his corpse being stolen, that he had himself buried in the bank's vaults. A truly giant deposit! His spirit is believed to protect the bank from thieves.

One of the cashiers accidentally told her the whole sorry tale. She collapsed, unable to face the awful facts. The following day she came back and asked to see her brother. The kind cashier, recognising Sarah, escorted her home. The day after that Sarah returned. The cashier was very busy. He didn't want to upset Sarah so he just told her that her brother was not in today. Sarah nodded and wandered off. The next day she was back again.

Soon all the staff in the bank knew Sarah. As she always wore the same dark dress they nicknamed her the Black Nun. Each day at around noon she would arrive at the front counter and ask to speak to Peter. Every day she would receive the same reply: 'No, Madam, your brother is not in today.' (Though a few did mutter: 'Look, you mad old boot, he's been dead for ages. Isn't it time you found something else to do?')

She would nod, seeming to understand, slope off, and then return undeterred the very next day. Rain or shine she visited the bank for over forty years. When she died the bank paid for her funeral and she was buried next door in the churchyard of St Christopher-le-Stocks.

The churchyard is now the bank's garden. It is said that on misty mornings the shadowy figure of woman in a black dress can clearly be seen hurrying from the garden to the bank.

Cashiers have reported trying to serve an old lady dressed in black only for her to disappear before their eyes. One man, who was holding a door open for someone, was astonished to see a woman in Victorian dress coming toward the bank. He blinked and she was gone. It looks as though Sarah is still searching for her brother.

The Grey Lady of St Thomas's Hospital, Lambeth

St Thomas's Hospital is where the famous nurse Florence Nightingale founded her nursing school. To this day nurses at St Thomas's are called Nightingales. A mysterious spirit dressed in grey haunts the hospital.

Spooky City

Lambeth in South London used to be jam-packed with wizards, astrologers and fortune tellers. Simon Forman, the Elizabethan egghead and alchemist, lived there, as did the astrologer Francis Moore. Old Moore turned up his toes in 1715, but his Almanack, with its spooky predictions for the year ahead is still an annual bestseller.

The brilliant poet and painter William Blake lived in Lambeth in the 1790s. He once saw a ghost while strolling home one evening. He described the apparition as being 'scaly, speckled, very awful'. William saw rather a lot of strange things. When he was a nipper he claimed to see angels in a tree in Peckham! Some have suggested that William was a bit bonkers.

The grey lady first appeared at the hospital during the Second World War. In November 1943, parts of the hospital were completely destroyed by German bombs. One morning Charlie Bide, a hospital orderly, was clearing away some rubble caused by the previous night's attack. Picking his way through the fragments of fallen bricks he accidentally inhaled a lung full of dust and started coughing. He sat down to get his breath back and took a brief rest.

Charlie was tired; he'd had quite enough of Mr Hitler disturbing his sleep. The dust had dried his mouth out and he was just about to head off to the canteen for a nice cup of tea when he noticed something glinting. He discovered it was a mirror. By some miracle it had survived the blast completely intact. As Charlie admired his reflection he became aware of another figure looking back at him. There in the glass was a nurse wearing an old-fashioned grey uniform. She seemed to smile at him but there was something chilling about her. Her eyes were icy. Panic-stricken, Charlie dropped the mirror. When he picked it up again only his face stared back at him. He never saw the grey lady again but after the war, when the hospital was rebuilt, she became a regular visitor.

In the 1950s one nurse was busily filling water jugs when an elderly man announced that he didn't need any more as the other nurse had only just given him a glass of water.

'Yes, dear,' the nurse said. 'That'll be the army of invisible nurses who always help me on my rounds. Sorry, love, but I am the only one on duty this evening. Let's have no more of this nonsense. Come on, drink up, you know what the doctor said about keeping your fluids up.'

The man wouldn't be so easily fobbed off. Even when the nurse threatened to give him a bedbath (a nasty rub-down with a cold damp sponge) there and then, he still swore blind that a kindly looking nurse dressed all in grey had attended to him. Sadly the patient died the next day and the identity of the other nurse was never discovered.

A year later another patient in the same ward also claimed to have seen the grey lady. He saw the ghost warming its hands by a fire. Around this time a group of nurses were amazed to see a grey figure gliding past the front of the hospital.

There are many theories as to who the ghost was. Some claim she is the spirit of a nurse who killed herself after accidentally administering a fatal overdose. Others say the ghost is that of a nurse who committed suicide after a love affair ended. In either case her wispy form continues to stalk the wards.

The Unknown Soldier at Westminster Abbey

Ghostly legends swarm around Westminster Abbey. When the first church was built the apostle St Peter is said to have materialized and blessed the building. (Admittedly, they did drink quite a lot of communion wine that day!) More recent apparitions have included a hooded monk and a spectral vicar. Both have been seen quietly floating around the abbey.

One of the most famous tombs in the Abbey is that of the Unknown Soldier. The soldier, whose name was never discovered, died fighting in France during the First World War. The war ended at 11 o'clock on 11 November 1818. So his body was buried in the nave of the Abbey at 11 o'clock on 11 November 1920 to commemorate the millions who died in the conflict. Occasionally a mournful ghost dressed in an army uniform appears by the side of the tomb. Witnesses have stated the ghost seems just about to speak, perhaps to tell them his name, when his image blurs into nothing. We still don't know who he is.

CHAPTER SIX

Acting Up! Spooks on the Stage

Judging from the number of ghosts who haunt London's Theatre
Land death is not the final curtain.

Lights Out for Dan Leno of Drury Lane

The London music-hall performer Dan Leno was the Robbie
Williams of his day. A talented comic singer, dancer and all-
round entertainer, he was a huge star. His cheery personality
and comic brilliance endeared him to thousands. Dan started his
career as a clog dancer but he soon left stomping around in big
shoes behind him. (I can't imagine it was very popular even then,
can you?) By 1901 he was touring America and sold out New
York's Music Hall. Later that year he returned to London in
triumph and appeared in a special performance for Edward, the
Prince of Wales.

Every year, from 1888 until 1903, he appeared in pantomime
at the Theatre Royal on Drury Lane. These shows were
incredibly popular. Huge queues for tickets blocked the street.
Those who didn't get in or couldn't afford to see the show milled
outside just hoping to catch a glimpse of Dan making his way to
the theatre.

Dan prided himself on never missing a performance but by 1903 he was exhausted and just after completing the pantomime season he suffered a complete breakdown. He was never the same again. He couldn't recognize members of his own family; he mistook them for characters from his stage act. He would bow to imaginary audiences and break into song when asked if he wanted his tea. He died in 1904. Enormous crowds attended his funeral procession. It was, however, not to be his final performance …

In the 1920s the actor Sydney Lupino was appearing in panto at the Theatre Royal. One evening Sydney was relaxing in his dressing room after a show. The audience had been particularly boisterous that night and now he had a headache. The cries of 'BEHIND YOU!' were still ringing in his ears and so he lay down on a couch and tried to get some sleep. He'd just dozed off when a rustling sound disturbed his slumbers. Assuming it was the caretaker Bernard, he boomed: 'Look, Bernard, can't you give me five minutes' peace? I am an artist, for heaven's sake! I need some rest, darling. How can I be expected to remember my lines when I am worn out?'

To his surprise his words were met with an eerie silence. He sat up. There, walking through his dressing room, was a pale, ghostly figure of a man. Flabbergasted, he tried to speak to it, only to see the phantom walk straight through the closed door and disappear. Jumping to his feet, he pulled the door open.

There was nothing there. He ran down the corridor and finally found Bernard mopping the floor near the auditorium.

' Er, Bernard, has anyone else been along this corridor?' Sydney asked cautiously.

'No, Mr Lupino. The others have all gone. Just the two of us now,' was Bernard's reply.

Shaking his head in disbelief, Sydney nervously returned to his room. It was empty. He suddenly noticed he hadn't removed his grease paint and so sat down in front of the mirror and began to wipe his face clean. The cleansing lotion cooled his face and he started to relax. Just then he became aware of another face in the mirror. There staring back at him was the familiar face of one of Drury Lane's greatest stars. It was none other than Dan Leno. Sydney sat transfixed as the face slowly faded away before his eyes. He didn't bother removing the rest of his make-up; quickly grabbing his coat and hat, he fled from the theatre in a state of utter terror.

He returned to the theatre the following day. He discovered that not only was that dressing room Dan Leno's personal favourite but that Dan had used it on the night of his very final performance. Sydney didn't see Dan again but his ghost was also known to haunt the Collins Music Hall in Islington. Apparently his spirit would watch rehearsals and if any actors gave bad performances he would click his spectral fingers or play with the lights. (Well, the theatre's director always blamed the disturbances on the ghost ... Umm, I wonder?) The Collins closed down years ago but Dan's ghost was once glimpsed dancing across Islington Green. So if you keep your eyes peeled you might just get to see the legendary Dan Leno after all.

The Theatre Royal's Grey Ghost

Dan Leno is not the only ghost to haunt the Theatre Royal on Drury Lane. The other resident phantom is also a theatre critic; the ghost only appears during runs of successful shows (it's rumoured to be very fond of musicals). The ghost doesn't seem to like late nights; in fact, the phantom has only ever been seen in the afternoons. (Perhaps even ghouls need their beauty sleep.) The ghost, a glowing grey figure who wears an old-fashioned hat with three corners (as worn by Dastardly Dick Turpin) and what looks like riding boots, strides along the circle (the seats above the stalls) and then vanishes into the wall at the far end of the theatre. No one knows exactly who the ghost is but a grim discovery in Victorian times gives us a clue to its identity.

In 1840, when the theatre was being renovated, a bricked-up room was discovered. Inside it was the decaying skeleton of a young man. His features had long rotted away but the remnants of cloth clinging to the bones looked like an old-fashioned riding outfit. Embedded in the skeleton's chest was a dagger. This man had evidently been murdered and his body then bricked up to prevent discovery. Who the man was or why he was murdered is still a mystery. Few doubt that he must be the theatre's grey ghost.

An Apparition at The Adelphi

Most theatres try to keep drama firmly on the stage. In 1897 the Adelphi on the Strand saw a real-life tragedy take place outside its doors. The leading actor, William Terriss, was murdered. His murderer was his co-star, Richard Prince. Now that really was a killer performance!

William was good-looking. He was also a brilliant actor whose talents were enjoyed by the public and admired by his fellow thespians. Dogs stopped barking when William walked by. Crying babies smiled when he drew near. The Covent Garden greengrocers gave him the freshest fruit. Everyone liked William. Well, everyone except Richard, that is. On that particular evening Richard snapped. He'd had enough of Mr Wonderful William Terriss, thank you very much. It just wasn't fair. He had all the best lines in the play. He had a bigger dressing room and his name was plastered all over the theatre. It was time for action. After the show Richard went round to the stage door. When William emerged he stabbed him to death with a dagger. At his trial, Richard was found to be barking mad and was locked away for the rest of his life.

William's ghost first appeared a couple of nights after his death. The phantom, which still lingers around the theatre to this day, is described as a tall willowy white figure resplendently dressed in a long cape, top hat and gloves. He tends to hover by the side of the stage. Actors regard his appearance as sign of good luck. How many of them use the stage door after he has visited is another question ...

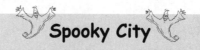

Spooky City

The Elizabethan playwright Christopher Marlowe was a dab hand at casting. He was holding auditions for his new play, *Dr Faustus*, a great story about a man who sells his soul to the Devil, when in walked an actor who looked absolutely perfect for the main part ...

'Name?' asked Marlowe.

'Lucifer Beelzebub Satan but friends just call me Nick,' replied the actor.

'Ah, right, er ... Nick. Let me see ... your last acting job was a three-month stint in the Miracle plays in Clerkenwell. Jolly good. Since then you've been teaching English as a foreign language and spreading evil and temptation throughout the globe. Great. My god! Are those your own horns?'

'Yes. The tail's real as well.'

'It's awfully good. Red really suits you. I originally had you down to audition for the hero but now I've met you, I think you'd make a brilliant villain. How do you fancy playing the Devil, Nick? It's a tough one, I know, but I get the sense this role was made for you.'

'I'd be delighted to give it a try,' said Nick.

' Welcome aboard. Rehearsals start 9 a.m. on Monday. See you then. What is that horrible farty smell?'

It probably didn't happened exactly like that but...

In 1593, during a production of *Dr Faustus* at the Bell Sauvage Inn Theatre on Ludgate Hill, audiences really did believe that the Devil had appeared on stage. People were so frightened that they fainted or broke into prayer whenever the actor playing the Devil appeared. (If it *was* an actor ...)

High Spirits at the Haymarket

From 1853 until his death in 1876, John Buckstone was the manager of the Theatre Royal on Haymarket, near Piccadilly. John was a jack of all theatrical trades. He acted, wrote and directed plays; he helped design the sets and even organized the publicity. His plays were always great successes. John was a workaholic and a bit of a control freak. He hardly ever left the theatre. It is not surprising that even from beyond the grave his can't help interfering. His ghost likes to make guest appearances just to see how things are going.

Like the grey man at Drury Lane, John's ghost is only supposed to appear when shows are going to be a hit. A faint whispering sound has disturbed actors in the dressing rooms. One leading lady, on hearing these strange murmurs, was shocked to see a tall white figure in a long, Victorian frock-coat peer in through the door. The spectre nodded slightly and then was gone. If John really likes the play his ghost has even been known to join in on stage!

CHAPTER SEVEN

Friendly Phantoms

Not all ghosts are doom, gloom and rattling chains; some seem to rather like the afterlife. They get to haunt their old haunts, stay out late on the town and generally enjoy themselves.

Sunny Days at Somerset House

The magnificent Somerset House on the Strand might be expected to harbour some gruesome ghosts or devilish phantoms. Lord Somerset, who first built a house there (and, yes, who it is named after), had his head chopped off by King Henry VIII. The house was once used as a morgue; the bodies of King James I and Oliver Cromwell were both stored there. This was where the extremely naughty Hellfire Club met and most sinister of all … it was once the Inland Revenue's head office!

Thankfully it is now home to the Courtauld art gallery. In the 1700s it was the headquarters of the Royal Navy. When he wasn't at sea, Lord Admiral Horatio Nelson (you know the one-eyed, one-armed, 'Kiss me Hardy' sailor with the big column in Trafalgar Square, oh for heaven's sake, just ask a pigeon) spent a great deal of time at Somerset House. After he was killed in the battle of Trafalgar on 21 October 1805, his body was shipped backed to the Royal Naval Hospital at Greenwich. He was then buried in St Paul's Cathedral.

On warm sunny mornings Nelson's ghost finds St Paul's a bit stuffy so he leaves his resting-place and takes a stroll to Tragalgar Square (what a big head) and then drifts down to Somerset House. His spectre, often seen walking across the courtyard, is always described as looking a little pale (wouldn't you if you'd been dead for 200 years?) but very happy. From here his ghost (with its one good eye) can watch the boats on the Thames; maybe they remind him of his own great sea voyages. Sometimes he can be heard cheerfully whistling a little nautical ditty as he walks along.

All Smiles at the Ship Tavern

The Ship Tavern is landlocked in the very heart of Holborn. This doesn't seem to bother the pub's resident spook, though. The impish ghost is one of London's friendliest phantoms. He or she doesn't go in for chain-rattling or spine-chilling screams. No, this ghost likes nothing more than to give the bar a warm glow. When nobody is about it delights in hiding the cellar keys and moving bottle openers and cutlery around.

In the 1500s the pub was used by Catholics to hold secret masses; so it's possible that the jovial ghost could be a Catholic priest executed by Queen Elizabeth I. The ghost could, however, be an old customer who has just chosen to ignore the very final call for last orders.

The Devil's Kitchen

Delightful Recipes for You to Create Great Ghost Stories of Your Own.

Ingredients

You will need the following ingredients to create a tasty terrifying tale to scare your friends:

A dark and stormy night

A foggy morning

A black cape (or an anorak)

An old prison, castle, palace or pub

An ancient murder, execution or suicide

A shadowy figure

A shifty-looking butler, barman, lord of the house or guard.

A dark shape

Knocking sounds

An icy sensation

Drips of blood

Rattling chains

A blood sucking vampire

A werewolf

Gary Barlow

Drunk as a Lord

Lord Angosteen was a dandy, the eighteenth century's version of a fashion victim. Angosteen wore the silliest and most expensive clothes. Frilly collars, velvet suits, bizarre buckled shoes – you name it, he wore it. Before going out to the Ship and Billet Inn in Greenwich each night, he would spend ages getting ready. His butler Carstairs was a patient man but sometimes even he was shocked by quite how long it took his master to get dressed. Despite his elaborate and appalling dress sense Angosteen was a generous and jolly man. He had loads of friends and went to parties almost every night. He usually rolled home at dawn drunkenly singing his head off - much to the annoyance of his neighbours on Shooter's Hill in Blackheath.

About thirty years ago a milkman near Blackheath was going about his rounds. He'd popped a couple of bottles on the step of a house on Vanbrugh Hill and was just making his way back to his float. As he turned into the road he met an extraordinary sight. There, gliding before him, was a ghostly coach. It looked so

real that the milkman could even see steam rising from the nostrils of the horses who pulled it along. From inside the phantom carriage he heard a man, drunkenly singing away. He stood and watched the coach until its image shimmered and disappeared. Angosteen, it appears, was still up to his old antics.

CHAPTER EIGHT

Help, Mummy!

The Curse of the Casket in the British Museum

There are many strange stories about ancient Egyptian curses. The most famous is that of King Tutankamun; nearly all of those who discovered the ancient tomb of the King are said to have died in mysterious circumstances. The British Museum experienced some very odd events of its own when it took possession of an Egyptian casket …

The casket is supposed to have been brought to England by the keen amateur Egyptologist Douglas Murray.

In 1888 Douglas was staying in Cairo with his friends, Alex and Julian. They had all travelled to Egypt to buy ancient artefacts. (It was the Victorian answer to backpacking.) Within a couple of days they were approached by a dealer in antiquities (very old stuff) who claimed to have something that might interest them. The man took them to a small shop that smelt of goats. (Nice!) It was full of broken bits of pottery, old carpets and cheap trinkets. Just as the men were about to make their excuses and leave, he led them into a back room. Here lay a beautifully decorated casket. The dealer proudly announced that this was a very rare piece. The case, he said, had belonged to a High Priestess of the Temple of Amen Re.

Douglas was entranced, although he had no idea who Amen Re was. The casket was so beautiful he would have bought it even if he had discovered Re had been the god of cheese-graters.

'Cash or cheque?' Douglas stuttered.

'Only cash,' the man swiftly replied.

They agreed a price and Douglas arranged to have the casket shipped back to his London home.

Later that day the three friends met for dinner in their hotel. Alex claimed to feel unwell and went to bed early. The next day they had all planned to go duck shooting on the Nile. Alex was still sick and so Douglas and Julian went without him. Fortunately for our feathered friends, Douglas and Julian weren't very good shots. The pair were happily firing away when Julian's gun suddenly exploded. The blast shattered the bones in his right arm. Julian collapsed on the deck, his damaged arm flapping about like a piece of seaweed.

A doctor trussed the arm up in a splint but somehow the limb had become infected and Julian died of blood poisoning two days later. In the meantime Alex had slipped into a fever and was now writhing about in bed. In moments of consciousness he kept muttering about the casket. A day later he too was dead. Douglas decided he'd had quite enough of Egypt and caught the first boat home.

Arriving back some weeks later he was surprised to find the casket waiting for him. He examined it with some trepidation. Looking at it, he was once more struck by its beauty. The notion of a deadly curse seemed ridiculous in the cool London air. Damn it, he thought, this is England in the 19th century. What on earth had gotten into him? Julian and Alex's deaths were terrible tragedies but they were unfortunate accidents, nothing more.

Spooky City

The ancient Egyptians weren't the only to people to mummify dead bodies. In 1832 the body of the London-born thinker and scientist Jeremy Bentham was mummified. Jeremy's mummy is on display at University College on Gower St in London.

Unfortunately the London embalmers botched the job. Jeremy's head started to go mouldy and had to be replaced with a waxwork copy! Jeremy's ghost takes revenge by moving books and rustling papers in the university library.

A month passed and nothing odd had happened. Douglas relaxed. He even held a small dinner party to show off the casket. Margaret, a journalist friend who shared an interest in Ancient Egypt, came along. She asked if she might borrow it for a few nights, she wanted to have a go at deciphering the hieroglyphs etched on to its surface. Douglas agreed.

Two weeks later Douglas returned home to find Margaret's fiancé waiting for him. He was extremely distressed. Since the casket had come into Margaret's home, she had fallen ill and both of her dogs had died. Douglas was shocked but not surprised. When the casket returned he wasted no time in selling it to a collector in Streatham. (He didn't mention its deadly history.)

The collector fell ill just days after taking possession of the casket. A friend, who was a medium, told him to get rid of it. He donated it to the British Museum.

When the casket arrived at the British Museum in Bloomsbury, two porters were sent to carry it into the building. One tripped and broke his arm. Not a good omen. Once inside, the casket was taken to be photographed. The photographer died in strange circumstances within days of taking the shot. A catalogue of accidents soon grew around the casket: museum guards claimed to feel ill if they were stationed anywhere near it; visitors fainted in front of it and strange noises were also reported. People became so scared they stopped visiting the museum. In 1921 two psychics were called in. They performed an exorcism on the casket and for the last eighty years Amen Re has been at peace. The case is still on show in the museum today.

There is, however, another story ... some claim that the casket now held in the museum is a different one. They maintain that the museum authorities had grown tired of Douglas's troublesome casket and in 1912 they decided to loan it to a museum in New York. The casket was sent to Southampton were it was loaded onto a ship bound for America. The ship's name was the *RMS Titanic* and we all know what happened to that ...

Spooky City

Not far from the British Museum is Gordon Square. For centuries it was a swampy field full of pigs and young men fighting duels. Duelling with swords or pistols was considered an honourable way to settle arguments. (At least someone had the last word; unfortunately it was usually, 'Urg … I am dying.')

Two brothers are supposed to have killed one another in a duel in the field. They had both fallen in love with the same girl and fought to decide who should marry her. Asking the girl would have been far too easy. Years after the duel their footprints remained eerily preserved in the soggy ground. The area became known as the Field of the Forty Footsteps because in a duel the opponents walk twenty paces apart before they start fighting.

Old Jimmy Garlick

Garlick Hill is just opposite Southwark Bridge (just by London Bridge Station). It was where delightfully whiffy bulbs of garlic used to be sold. (No vampires in that neighbourhood!) The local church, St James, Garlickhythe, was burnt to a crisp in 1666 during the Great Fire of London. (Not so great if your house was burned down!) In 1682 it was rebuilt by Christopher Wren (Mr St Paul's Cathedral strikes again.) By the 1830s it was looking shabby and so repairs were carried out. Builders uncovered a very weird glass coffin. Inside the coffin was something even weirder: a mummy. The ancient Britons and the Romans did occasionally mummify very important people. This mummy might have been a king or a warrior (or a very successful garlic salesman). He could even have been the very first Lord Mayor of London, as six Lord Mayors were buried here.

The mummy, nicknamed Old Jimmy Garlick, was put on display in a glass case in the church and for a hundred years he sat there minding his own business. During an air raid in the Second World War, though, a bomb hit the church, shattering his case.

Jimmy was furious. It was bad enough being dragged from a nice grave and gawked at every day but this, this was the last straw. There was nothing else for it. From now on, haunting would be Jimmy Garlick's game.

True to his word, Jimmy's phantom has roamed the church ever since. Priests and parishioners have been disturbed by the flickering shape of a man standing next to the altar. The shape appears to be praying but if anyone approaches, it instantly melts away. An American tourist was stunned to see a forlorn-looking white spectre marching up the Nave toward him. The phantom gave off an odd pulsing glow. It was gaunt, almost skeletal. The tourist couldn't describe its face but said that its eyes blazed like flashlights. Before he could attract anyone else's attention the spook had gone.

CHAPTER NINE

Monarch Manifestations

The names of the kings and queens of England adorn London's roads, streets, parks and squares. Their palaces remain some of the city's finest buildings. London has seen monarchs overthrown, murdered and, just once, executed. It is not surprising that the city has more than its fair share of sovereign spooks.

George the Ghostly German

King George II became King of England in 1727 when his dad, King George I, died. (The English royal family has never been very imaginative when it comes to names!) George (II) didn't like England. He was born in Hanover in Germany and oh, how he wished he'd stayed there. He hated the English weather, he didn't like the food and he found the beer absolutely undrinkable.

To be fair to George, his father, King George I, was even worse. George Senior detested England so much that he spent as little time here as possible.

In the last days of his life George II was confined to Kensington Palace. Although he was very ill, George would get up every morning to see if there was any news from his beloved

Hanover. Each day he was bitterly disappointed; poor winds had delayed ships travelling from Europe. He spent hours staring at the palace's weather vane, hoping for a sign that the winds had changed. He died just two days before the ships arrived.

On calm days George's ghost returns to keep watch on the weather vane. Palace officials have spotted the old king pacing backwards and forwards like a penguin. He tugs at his wig, sending up a cloud of white powder, and repeatedly mutters, 'Warum nicht kommen sie?' (Why don't they come?) After one last mournful glance at the vane, his dejected-looking spectre hobbles away. He's probably still annoyed about being stuck in England.

The Ginger Queen in Greenwich

The Tudor monarchs adored Greenwich. Henry 'Head Count' VIII, 'Bloody' Mary I and Elizabeth I were all born in the splendid royal palace there. In Tudor times much of central London was a disease-ridden cesspool. Greenwich (green by name, green by nature) was a convenient rural retreat for the royal family.

Greenwich Palace was Queen Elizabeth I's favourite house. It was in the palace grounds that Sir Walter Raleigh plonked his cloak over a puddle so the queen wouldn't get her feet wet. Yes, Elizabeth had some great times in Greenwich; she even signed Mary Queen of Scots' death warrant here. Off with her head!

The Royal Naval College stands on the site of Elizabeth's old palace. (King Charles II had planned to build a new palace at Greenwich but he died before it was finished.) Elizabeth's palace may have gone but Elizabeth pops by now and again. (She was always very keen on sailors!) An elegant white spectre, with a shock of frizzy red hair, has been spied walking across the college courtyard. The ghostly queen hates being approached so if you do see her make sure you keep your distance.

CHAPTER TEN

The Most Haunted House in London

Number 50, Berkeley Square in Mayfair was once London's most haunted house. Its reputation was so fearsome that few dared even to walk past its door. The horror writer M R James wrote about it in a chilling ghost tale called *The Summer School*. The unruly spirits have been silent for nearly a hundred years but who knows, one day they just might return.

Berkeley Square's fine houses were built in the 1740s. Elegant and fashionable, they were highly desirable properties. For a time the then Prime Minister George Canning lived at Number 50. Unearthly occurrences appear to have dogged the house since its earliest days. Some occupants claimed to have heard a girl shrieking; others recalled the sound of a body being dragged down the stairs. Passers-by maintained they saw a wispy, hazy light flickering in the upstairs windows. The house became so notorious that people were too frightened to live there. No one seemed to know who or what was haunting the house or why.

One man who thought the whole thing was utter rubbish was the twenty-year-old dandy, Sir Robert Warboys. Robert was enjoying a pint or two with friends in a pub in Holborn when someone mentioned the eerie events at Berkeley Square. 'Unadulterated poppycock' was Robert's verdict. (It must be added he had drunk a lot of beer by this time and was tipsy.) His friend weren't so sure. 'Well,' he said, waving a foaming tankard in the air, spilling beer all over his trousers in the process, 'I'll prove it. I will stay in the house all night just to show you there is no ghost.' A carriage was hired and the party made off for Mayfair. Arriving at the house they forced the door open and staggered in.

On the short journey they had all been laughing and joking about the ghost but now standing in the hallway they fell silent. The house was icy cold. Robert didn't appear to notice. He pulled out a pistol, burbled something about firing a shot if he saw anything and marched up the stairs. His friends were too scared to stay in the house. They lay down on the grass outside and fell asleep. Just after one o'clock in the morning they were woken by a gunshot that echoed through the square. Startled, they stumbled to their feet and rushed into Number 50. They raced upstairs and there in the corner of one of the bedrooms was

Robert's lifeless body. A look of unimaginable fear was frozen on his face. His features were twisted like a grotesque waxwork dummy; his lips were curled, his eyes stared blankly into space and a smoking pistol was clutched in his right hand. A bullet was lodged in the wall opposite him. Whatever had caused his ghastly death was nowhere to be seen.

The house, unsurprisingly, remained empty. A couple of years after Robert's death two sailors from Portsmouth – Eddie Blunden and Bob Martin – had an equally ghastly experience in 50 Berkeley Square.

Like Robert, Eddie and Bob had been enjoying a night on the town. Having spent all their money on drink they were looking for a park bench or an unattended shed where they could sleep. Wandering from Ye Grapes pub into Berkeley Square they spotted the 'To Let' sign on Number 50. They broke in and settled down for the night, tickled pink with their good fortune. Eddie was having a brilliant dream about a desert island packed with beautiful mermaids and bottles of rum when he woke up with a start. He couldn't feel his arms. He yelled out to Bob but a mysterious force strangled his cries. Now he found that he couldn't breathe. A disgusting wispy figure was crouching over him. What looked like hands were clamped around his throat. The creature was squeezing the life out of him. He flailed at the spectre with his legs but his feet passed straight through it. Bob tried to help his friend but as he approached the monster he recoiled in terror. He ran from the house and managed to find a policeman.

The policeman, confronted with a drunken sailor babbling about ghosts, was bemused. As the sailor was clearly petrified he agreed to investigate. (What else could you do with a drunken sailor?) When they reached the house a diabolical sight awaited them. There, perched on top of the front railings, was Eddie. He appeared to have jumped or been pushed out of the upper-floor windows. A spike on the railings had pierced his chest. Blood was gently dripping down on to the pavement below.

The ghost had claimed its second victim.

Who could this murderous ghost be?

One possibility is a Mr Myers who lived at Number 50 in the early 1800s. Myers is supposed to have rented the house just before his marriage. He was young, rich and deeply in love. He spent a fortune on having it redecorated. He bought a wardrobe full of new clothes for his bride. In one room he built a nursery, jammed full of toys, for the family they planned to start.

On the eve of the wedding his cooks worked through the night preparing a vast banquet for all the guests. The next day he got up early, bursting with excitement. He crept into the kitchen and admired the wedding cake and the array of freshly baked pies. Delighted, he went back upstairs to get ready. He arrived at the altar and stood waiting for his bride to appear. An hour passed and still she had not arrived. Two hours passed. Myers' palms itched, he felt queasy and anxious. Where was she? A thousand mad ideas flooded into his head. Had she been involved in an accident? Had she been kidnapped by pirates whilst on her way to the church? Perhaps even now she was tied to the mast of a galleon bound for the South Seas. The guests were getting restless. The vicar, who'd been looking forward to a large glass of sherry after the service, glanced at his watch and tutted. Half an hour later a note calling the wedding off arrived.

Myers was shattered. When he returned to Berkeley Square he ordered his servants not to touch a thing. He went to bed.

From then onwards he was never seen during the day. At night he took a meal in his room and then paced the upper floors of the house until dawn. The beautiful banquet slowly rotted away. Rats finished off the cake and had a good go at the pies until a butler, unable to stand the smell any longer, threw them out. Moths nibbled at the dresses in the wardrobe. The toys in the nursery became coated in a thick layer of dust.

Myles died just a few years later. His body was found slumped in an upstairs room. He had suffered a massive heart attack; his heart really had broken. He was still dressed in his wedding suit.

What the Dickens?

Myles may have inspired Charles Dickens – the author of *A Christmas Carol* – to create Miss Haversham in another classic, *Great Expectations*. In the book Miss Haversham is also jilted and wears her wedding dress for the rest of her life. The character was partly based on an old woman he remembered from childhood but Dickens – a huge fan of London myths and ghosts stories – would certainly have heard all about Berkeley Square.

In 1971 Dickens's own ghost made a brief appearance outside his old home in Clerkenwell, 48 Doughty St. The writer's ghostly figure, wearing a top hat, strolled up the road and promptly disappeared, never to be seen again.

Bizarre lights and strange sounds are rumoured to have started shortly after Myles's death.

There might, however, be a less ghoulish explanation for the ghosts.

Number 50 was once home to a gang of forgers. They skulked about at night, printing bank notes and generally getting up to no good. The neighbours were getting suspicious. Some went round to complain.

'An Englishman's home may well be his castle,' they said, 'but clanking around at odd hours – in what sounds like armour - is just not on, lads.'

'Sorry,' said the gang, 'it's not really our fault. It's the house, you see; it's haunted. We'll try and have a word with them but you know ghosts, once they start rattling those chains there's no stopping them.'

The neighbours didn't believe them. The following night they called the police. The police found the gang hard at work printing £10 notes. The gang were flung into Newgate Gaol and later hanged. The gang may have gone but the ghost story stuck. Before long nearly everyone in the square said they had seen it or knew someone else who had ...

Maggs Bookshop now occupies the house. No ghosts have been seen for years. Every so often, though, customers do claim to feel an odd icy sensation while they are browsing.

Well, our ghostly tour is at an end but I hope you've enjoyed reading about London's grim ghouls, fiendish phantoms and scary spooks. Whether you believe in ghosts or not, there is certainly something magical about London. The next time you're in the city keep your eyes peeled, perhaps you might spot a strange shape or get the feeling you are not alone ...

Spooky Sites to Visit

The Tower of London, Tower Hill, London EC3. Royal palace, prison and place of execution, the Tower is a top place to visit. The Beefeater Guards give marvellous tours. www.toweroflondontour.com

The Bank of England Museum, Threadneedle St, London EC2. If you are lucky you might catch a glimpse of the Black Nun but if not, the bank's museum reveals what happens to your pocket money. www.bankofengland.co.uk

The Clink Prison Museum, 1 Clink Street, London SE1. The creepy museum of the prison 'that gave its name to all others' has a delightful collection of torture devices. www.clink.co.uk

The London Dungeon, 28-34 Tooley St, London SE1. This is London's most terrifying tourist spot. Explore grim torture chambers, watch horrible executions, trail Jack the Ripper's gruesome murders, come face to face with foul figures from the past and even get sentenced to death! www.thedungeons.com

St James Garlickhythe Church, Garlick Hill, London, EC2. Old Jimmy Garlick's lair! Unfortunately Jimmy is no longer on display but you can soak up the church's wonderful atmosphere. www.stjamesgarlickhythe.co.uk

The Old Bailey Law Courts, Old Bailey, London EC1. A plaque commemorates the former site of Newgate Prison – home to the horrible Black Dog ...

Christ Church, Newgate St, London EC1. The ghostly greyfriars have been sighted here.

The Museum of London, 150 London Wall, London EC2. This brilliant museum has a recreation of a Newgate Gaol cell and it's packed full of great stuff on London. www.museum-london.org.uk

The Clerkenwell House of Detention, Clerkenwell Close, London EC1, is wonderful. This spooky underground museum gives a frightening taste of prison life.

Dickens House Museum, 48 Doughty Street, London WC1. Full of the famous ghost fan's possessions. You can imagine yourself transported back to the 1830s. www.dickensmuseum.com

Dennis Severs' House, 18 Folgate Street, Spitalfields, London EC1. This Georgian house – a living museum to the past – is extraordinarily spooky. It is inhabited by a fictional ghostly family - the Jervises. It isn't always open, so check on the website. www.dennisservershouse.co.uk

Gordon Square, London WC1. This elegant square was once the Ghostly Field of Forty Steps.

The British Museum, Great Russell Street, London WC1. Amen Re's spooky casket is housed on the first floor in the Egyptian room. www.thebritishmuseum.ac.uk

Somerset House, Strand, London WC2. Now open to public, this former Government office building has a beautiful courtyard of dancing water jets - just the thing to encourage old sea dog Nelson's ghost to put in an appearance. It also converts into an ice rink in the winter! www.somerset-house.org.uk

12 Buckingham St, London WC2. The diarist Samuel Pepys' old house is marked with a plaque. See if you can spy his spook in the upper-floor window.

Maggs Bookshop, 50 Berkeley Square, London W1. This great bookshop was once the most haunted house in London.

Kensington Palace, Kensington Gardens, W8. Tour this lovely royal residence and watch out for George II's ghost. www.hrp.org.uk

Holland House, Holland Park, London W11. Most of headless Henry's house was bombed in the Second World War but Holland Park is still a beautiful place in which to wander. A portrait of Henry Rich hangs in the Civil War room of the National Portrait Gallery, 2 St Martin's Place, London, WC2.

Waterstone's, 11 Islington Green, London N1. This bookstore is on the site of the old Collins Music Hall, once haunted by Dan Leno. Why not buy some more wonderful Watling Street books!

Parliament Hill and Hampstead Heath. Stroll on the beautiful Heath, view the whole of London from Parliament Hill and watch out for the ghosts of Dick Turpin and the Gunpowder Plotters.

Highgate Cemetery, Swains Lane, London N6. Keep an eye out for David Devant on Swains Lane, take a stroll in the eastern side and say hello to Karl Marx. The guided tour of the really scary western side is essential for any serious ghosthunter. www.highgatecemetery.co.uk

Pond Square, Highgate, London, N6. No chickening out! Hunt for Francis Bacon's ghostly bird.

The Original London Walk, P.O. Box 1708, London NW6. This company runs loads of wonderful ghost walks around the city. www.walks.com

If you enjoyed this book, why not try others in the series:

CRYPTS, CAVES AND TUNNELS OF LONDON
by Ian Marchant
Peel away the layers under your feet and discover
the unseen treasures of London beneath the streets.
ISBN 1-904153-04-6

GRAVE-ROBBERS, CUT-THROATS AND POISONERS
OF LONDON
by Helen Smith
Dive into London's criminal past and meet some of its
thieves, murderers and villains.
ISBN 1-904153-00-3

DUNGEONS, GALLOWS AND SEVERED HEADS OF LONDON
by Travis Elborough
For spine-chilling tortures and blood-curdling punishments,
not to mention the most revolting dungeons and prisons you
can imagine.
ISBN 1-904153-03-8

THE BLACK DEATH AND OTHER PLAGUES OF LONDON
by Natasha Narayan
Read about some of the most vile and rampant diseases ever
known and how Londoners overcame them – or not!
ISBN 1-904153-01-1

RATS, BATS, FROGS AND BOGS OF LONDON
by Chris McLaren
Find out where you can find some of the amazing species
London has to offer the budding naturalist.
ISBN 1-904153-05-4

In case you have difficulty finding any Watling St books in your local bookshop, you can place orders directly through

BOOKPOST
Freepost
PO Box 29
Douglas
Isle of Man
IM99 1BQ

Telephone: 01624 836000
e-mail: bookshop@enterprise.net